Stop Feeling
LAZY

Stop Feeling LAZY

How To BREAK The PROCRASTINATION Cycle Once & For All And EXCEL

By Carol Look

Copyright © 2013 Velocity House Publishing and Carol Look.

ALL RIGHTS RESERVED WORLDWIDE.

All rights reserved. No part of this document may be reproduced or transmitted in any form, either by electronic or mechanical means including information storage and retrieval systems without the prior written permission of the publisher. The only exception is for a reviewer who may quote brief passages in the review.

This publication is presented to you for informational purposes only and is not a substitution for any professional advice. The contents herein are based on the views and opinions of the author and all associated contributors.

While every effort has been made by the author and all associated contributors to present accurate and up to date information within this document, it is apparent technologies rapidly change. Therefore, the author and all associated contributors reserve the right to update the contents and information provided herein as these changes progress. The author and/or all associated contributors take no responsibility for any errors or omissions if such discrepancies exist within this document.

The author and all other contributors accept no responsibility for any consequential actions taken, whether monetary, legal, or otherwise, by any and all readers of the materials provided. It is the reader's sole responsibility to seek professional advice before taking any action on their part.

Readers results will vary based on their skill level and individual perception of the contents herein, and thus no guarantees, monetarily or otherwise, can be made accurately. Therefore, no guarantees are made.

ISBN: 978-1-62409-006-6

Contents

Introduction		1
Chapter 1	Little In Life Is More Intimidating Than A Blank Page	5
Chapter 2	Paying For Procrastination	8
Chapter 3	Elimination	16
Chapter 4	Why Procrastinate?	20
Chapter 5	Introduction to Meridian Tapping	29
Chapter 6	An in-Depth Look at EFT	37
Chapter 7	Sample Exercises	53
Chapter 8	Homework	70

Introduction

You stare at your computer screen in utter dismay. The empty document on your computer stares back. Desperate to type literally anything, you frantically reach for the keyboard and type the date at the top of the page. Satisfying that need, you move the cursor down two lines and prepare to really start writing.

Nothing. Your brain is in gridlock again. Absentmindedly you open up your favorite website and start browsing. Ten minutes later, guiltily, you close the window and go back to staring at the blank document. Still nothing.

"Maybe I'll just go for a walk," you say. You silently debate the idea for a moment, then push back your chair and stand. "Yeah, I'll go for a walk. It's a nice day, and I could use the air..."

You walk out of the room. Behind you, glaring at your receding back with unbridled accusation, is the bright, white screen of your abandoned computer. It's the white of blank documents, of looming deadlines and pressing workloads.

It's the white of procrastination.

"Due tomorrow? Do tomorrow." This is a simple creed to live by, and yet one that is increasingly problematic as you take on more and more responsibilities. It is a conundrum that constantly has you torn between stress and a *laissez-faire* attitude, where nothing gets done to its full potential and some projects don't get done at all.

As if your computer's accusations weren't enough, you notice even more symptoms of your procrastination as you walk through the house: the four-day-old pile of dishes in the sink, the game of Jenga that is on your trashcan. The cabinets that are so barren that an innocent bystander

Get Your FREE 40 Minute Tapping Session: *http://velocityhousepresents.com/stop-procrastinating*

might think someone stole all your food. The guitar you got for Christmas, the one you swore you'd learn, only to be condemned to a dusty corner of the living room, because you were too afraid people might laugh at you. A book on dieting and exercise sits on your coffee table. You picked it up for New Years last year, but never cracked it open, because it seemed like a chore. Besides, why diet and potentially rock the boat? You like the way you are. Even your clothes are a stark reminder of your bad habits-you put them on this morning, because they were the last of the clean clothes in your closet.

At this point, you know it's likely that you've spent more time procrastinating about most of these tasks than it would have taken you to just go ahead and complete them. If that's the case, why do you avoid them? It's like your brain is holding you back or trying to protect you from something.

"Still, maybe a walk really *would* do me good," you rationalize. You bargain with yourself. "I'll take a walk, and then I'll really get working. For real this time."

Yet when you return from your walk, it's time for more excuses. You make excuses all night, in fact, and then it's time to sleep.

Now, lying in bed and feeling incredibly guilty and stressed, you worry about the future. The deadline for your work is only days away, and your boss is going to expect two weeks of work. You've heard your boss give a good tongue-lashing before. The prospect of having one directed at you and your own work is paralyzing.

Then there are all those other projects caught in perpetual limbo. At least tomorrow's your day off. Maybe you can spend that day finishing up some of this work...

Yes, that settles it. You'll wake up early tomorrow morning and at least start a load of laundry and take out the trash. Then, you'll go sit at the computer and make a legitimate effort at your boss's project. There's only four days until your deadline. You can make it. It might be a bit stressful at the end, but it will get done without pulling any all-nighters. After that, you can swing by the grocery store, pick up a healthy dinner to start your diet, and be back in time to have a little free time. Who knows, maybe you'll even pick up that guitar again.

Your brain, satisfied that it's done its work and gotten your life back on track, shuts down.

Morning arrives, and your alarm goes off like an air raid siren. Blearily, you stretch and open your eyes. You think of the trash, the laundry, your boss's project, dieting, your guitar...

You hit the snooze button.

How long have you lived with procrastination? How long has it been holding you back from your full potential and causing you stress in both your work and home relationships?

It doesn't matter what you answer. Whether it's one day, one year, a decade, or your entire life-any amount of time is too long. Don't let procrastination monopolize your time any longer. You deserve a productive and abundant life. The easiest way to accomplish that? Simply keep reading.

Get Your FREE 40 Minute Tapping Session: *http://velocityhousepresents.com/stop-procrastinating*

Chapter 1

Little In Life Is More Intimidating Than A Blank Page

At least, that's how I used to feel before beginning a book. It's just a bunch of white space, an empty plane in need of words. As George Orwell, author of *1984,* once said, "Writing a book is a horrible, exhausting struggle, like a long bout of some painful illness."

The ultimate danger of procrastination is that it hits even the best of us, and it catches us entirely unaware. By the time we realize we're procrastinating, we're liable to find we've wasted too much time already. I used to find myself on many a morning opening up a blank document, typing a sentence or two, and then wandering off to go for a walk or make myself breakfast.

I never felt like I was procrastinating, simply because I was so "busy" all the time. It took me a few days to realize that, no, I did not deserve to take a break just because I wrote a heading at the top of the page. There's definitely not enough time in the day to get work done if you don't allow yourself the time to sit down and do it in the first place. My excuses to myself became more and more elaborate as the days went by, making little progress on my work. I even started avoiding my desk, because I knew I'd feel guilty about not working.

Get Your FREE 40 Minute Tapping Session: *http://velocityhousepresents.com/stop-procrastinating*

Surely work could wait until tomorrow. Today, I just needed to go grocery shopping, clean the house or organize my desk drawers. Then I'd notice how nice it was outside, and wonder how could I possibly waste such a gorgeous day sitting inside and working? Everything I did was objectively "productive," but none of it related to what I was actually supposed to be working on. I'm sure you can see the problem.

I also know that you've been there before. Let the person who has never procrastinated cast the first stone. The rest of us will just delay casting that stone until the last minute, then frantically cast as many stones as possible until one sticks.

With a big project looming on the horizon, you feel helpless in taking action, even as that distant horizon encroaches at a terrifying pace. Suddenly that big project on the horizon is towering over you, and you find yourself scrambling. It's one of the worst feelings in the world, yet we can't seem to break the habit.

It's a huge problem, regardless of what field you're in. Whether you're a student, an aspiring (or accomplished) artist, a tech whiz or a literal rocket scientist, procrastination is bound to strike at the worst possible time. It's even a problem in your personal life. You're just as apt to procrastinate on life's little chores-cleaning, dieting, exercising-as you are to procrastinate on the big projects.

Procrastination is an epidemic, seeking to rob the world of productivity.

The point is, it happens to everyone. Lucky for me, I learned how to eliminate my own procrastination. After all, it would be pretty ironic if I procrastinated writing a book about procrastination.

Before this book is over, you'll know how to combat your own procrastination tendencies and find the motivation to write your own book or paint your masterpiece, mow the lawn or whatever it is you continually put off until later.

What is your "blank page?" What are you procrastinating? Knowing some people, it may be easier for you to tally up what things you *haven't* procrastinated about, and that's fine. Only by admitting our procrastination can we eliminate it. As I said, it happens to even the best of us. It's a natural response, and one that you will grow to understand as you read this book. We're going to take a good look at what procrastination is, how it affects us and most importantly, how to eliminate it.

What would you do with an extra hour per day? Unless you're already overwhelmed, that extra hour

probably already exists. That hour could be yours every single day. All that's required is using your time more efficiently than you have been.

Chapter 2

Paying For Procrastination

"Procrastination" has a bad reputation, as well it should, but have you ever stopped to consider how procrastination is affecting you? It's one of those concepts we all instinctively recognize as a bad habit to get into, but I think we rarely analyze its effect on our life from a deeper standpoint.

Indeed, many of us are so used to delaying our tasks, that it almost becomes a comforting idea. I know plenty of people who say they work better when the deadline has almost caught up to them, or who claim to do their best work "under pressure." It's a film cliche at this point: the hero who expertly brings everything together in a neat package and prevents everything from collapsing at the last moment, turning the plot around and saving the day. I've even met a few of these miracle workers, and they certainly are a wonder to see.

Even they are suffering because of procrastination. The costs of avoiding a project are extensive and are not always so obvious. The most damaging effects won't come to fruition for years to come. It's worthwhile to quit your procrastination *now* to save yourself a whole lot of trouble. Habitually eliminating the mental blockage of this bad habit will have far-reaching repercussions, even beyond what you may consciously acknowledge or understand.

Get Your FREE 40 Minute Tapping Session: *http://velocityhousepresents.com/stop-procrastinating*

After years of working with people to eliminate their procrastination, I've found that the principle costs can easily be classified into three main categories: time, money and stress. There's a bit of overlap between the three groups, but overall, I find this is the most productive way to present the negative effects of procrastination.

Time

This category is almost too obvious. Of course procrastination is costing us time. That's the whole point! If it didn't cost us time, it wouldn't even be an issue. It wouldn't even be a concept.

Yet, I find that it is important to quantify the effects that procrastination has on our time, because it's often a sobering experience to face what we take for granted. We all "know" that procrastination costs us time, but how? What is procrastination really doing that's so damaging?

First, and most apparent, is the time that we waste by procrastinating. This comes in two forms: actions that are actually wasteful and actions that are only wasteful in the guise of procrastination. For instance, many people have a bad habit of browsing the Internet when they're procrastinating or otherwise consuming something. While the act of consumption can occasionally be useful, most of the time it's purely an experience done for pleasure. It's something that we do for entertainment, rather than personal betterment.

I'm not saying that we should never consume anything, because entertainment isn't necessarily a bad thing. Rather, if you find yourself spending a lot of your time on entertainment, especially when you know that there are actual tasks you have to accomplish, the time is effectively wasted. You've frittered away countless hours on something that, at the end of the day, is not very productive. Again, everyone needs entertainment occasionally. Moderation is the key difference between wasting time on entertainment and indulging in it as a necessary part of life is simply a matter of degree.

Get Your FREE 40 Minute Tapping Session: http://velocityhousepresents.com/stop-procrastinating

Then there is the other type of procrastination: we are always "busy," and what we are doing is technically productive, but it is procrastination because we're putting off our real tasks.

This is a lot more subtle and infinitely more difficult to recognize. Am I cleaning the house because it actually needs to be cleaned, or just because I don't want to write my book? Did I organize my desk drawers because they are messy, or because it kept me from my real work for two hours? Why have I walked the dog six times already today?

These are all productive tasks. However, when they distract from priority tasks, however, they become a problem. Again, it's a matter of degrees. We all have errands to run and dishes to wash,

but did you really need to check ten things off of your weekly chore list the day before your project is due, prompting you to stay awake all night playing catch-up? While wasted time is in and of itself a tragedy, the loss of freedom is far more damaging.

Let's say you have an upcoming project that will take twenty-five total hours. For the sake of a simple analogy, let's just say your boss really wants you to write up some reports by the end of next week. You have ten days to complete twenty-five hours of work, the only work you have until it's all finished. Well that's only two and a half hours per day. Practically nothing!

The smart worker will look ahead in his or her upcoming schedule, establish blocks of time in which they have nothing to do and start working right away. Maybe Tuesday has a nice five-hour block in the afternoon to get the project off the ground. Wednesday, though, you've got errands to run, so you only schedule two hours of work. However, because you completed so much work on Tuesday, there's still plenty of allowance for a short workday. By doing a few hours every day, the project is done early and your boss is pleased. On Friday, the original deadline, a bunch of friends take an impromptu trip downtown, and you're able to go along.

The procrastinator, however, will delay until sometime next week. Tuesday will be a blur of hours wasted instead of worked, and

Wednesday your errands will still be the main focus. Suddenly, Thursday and Friday are entirely booked. It's going to take over twelve hours per day to get the project done on time, if you can even force yourself to work that long. If not, there may be an all-nighter or two in your future. To add insult to self-inflicted injury, you won't be able to tag along when your friends go out on Friday night. Instead, you will spend that time at home, working on your project while wishing that you were out having fun, causing resentment toward both the project and your own lax work habits.

This scenario, of course, is pretty low-stakes. It may not be a huge deal that you can't go out with friends on Friday night. After all, there's always next week. This is just an example, though I'm sure there have been higher-stakes examples in your own life where you had to miss something important because of work left to the last minute.

By properly managing your time, you can do your work on your own terms, when it best suits you. The freedom you attain in finishing a task sooner than expected is addicting. Think about how good you feel once you've gotten some bothersome task off your chest and how the world seems wide open. Now imagine that, by eliminating your procrastination, you could essentially have that feeling all the time.

It's liberating.

Money

If time is the most obvious cost associated with procrastination, surely money is the next distinct loss. On the other hand, the monetary deficits caused by procrastination are more complex than people often realize.

It starts with a mental blockage. One of the worst effects of procrastination is paralysis of your creativity. Not only do you feel like you are falling behind, but you can't even come up with an idea to get back on track. You won't be able to creatively build a new website or write a book or accomplish anything productive, really. You'll just feel like you're stuck in a rut.

Get Your FREE 40 Minute Tapping Session: *http://velocityhousepresents.com/stop-procrastinating*

In some circumstances, of course, there's a direct money-to-procrastination ratio. I've worked with numerous clients who are freelancers, including artists, writers and independent consultants, as well as small business owners, whose responsibility it is to keep their company afloat with their own work and effort.

These are the people who will lose the most money by procrastinating. Payment, in this case, is directly related to the completion of their work. By procrastinating, the freelancer endangers the success of the project and threatens the payment for their work. It's a simple relationship-one that we learned in elementary school, since receiving a good grade on a paper or a project is the grade school equivalent of this cost. "Get your work done; get rewarded." Still, there are less apparent costs that arise from the same issue.

Unless you're one of those miracle workers discussed above, your procrastination is probably damaging the quality of your work. Whatever task you set out to accomplish is going to get shorted, because you don't have the time to do it properly. Go ahead and ask a teacher whether or not they can see the difference between a paper written over the course of two weeks and one written the night before. If you rush a project, things will slip by. You'll make mistakes. Some of these errors will be tiny, not even worth a second glance. Instead of dotting every "i," maybe you only dotted half. Is it a huge problem? Probably not, but it is still an indication that you didn't take the work as seriously as it deserved. It's something that your employer may notice or something you look at later and regret.

Worse still are the huge errors. The ones that make you say, "How did I even do that?" Rushing through something means that you might not have the same presence of mind to pick up on errors, and you definitely won't have time to check over your work a second time. You've basically set up an environment that forces you to make errors, because you don't have time to look anything over to ensure quality.

How does this cost you money? It's actually costing you money in a number of different ways.

First of all, there's a good chance that you're going to have to fix those errors eventually. The best-case scenario is that the mistakes are simple to rectify, merely taking up more of your time. Since your time is worth something, you're still technically "losing" money, especially if you get paid a specific amount for a completed project regardless of how long it takes you.

The worst-case scenario is that your mistake ends up costing other people money, or worse, their jobs. This is especially true if you're running a small business. Make a large enough error, and you could sink your whole company-all because you put off a project too long and compounded the effects of your mistakes.

The long-term effects of procrastination are even harder to quantify, but no less scary. Every rushed project damages your credibility, no matter what position you fill in a company. A certain quality of work is expected from you, and a failure to deliver is going to hurt you down the line.

A freelancer who often procrastinates or turns in obviously-rushed work, for instance, may find themselves passed over in favor of other, similarly-skilled workers without a poor reputation. In many cases, the freelancer won't even know what they've done wrong. They'll either blame the company, or they'll move on without a second thought. Not only have they potentially called their payment for the current project into question, but they're indirectly damaging their future earning potential.

The same goes for hourly and salaried workers, however. Rushed or sloppy work is just as damaging, even when you have a steady job. Even when your job isn't called into question by negative performance reviews or angry bosses, you're definitely hurting your upwards mobility.

You'll be passed over for promotions or similar advancement opportunities because of your poor reputation amongst management. Just like the procrastinating freelancer, you've greatly damaged your future earning potential, perhaps without even realizing it. It's unlikely someone's going to tell you, "You aren't getting the promotion because you procrastinate too much," but it's not helping people's perception of you.

People are often great at recognizing procrastination in others. We all do it, so we all recognize the signs. Just like the parents who roll their eyes at their child who tries to get away with the same things the parents did years earlier, we all know when others are procrastinating.

The real challenge is recognizing our own procrastination habits before they become a problem in our work.

Stress

The least obvious, but most damaging, of procrastination costs arise from stress. Remember how I mentioned earlier that eliminating your procrastination and experiencing freedom of action is a liberating feeling. This is because you're digging yourself out from a stressful situation.

That feeling that it's "too late" to get your work done, that you wasted too much time or have met your match, is the most debilitating effect that procrastination has on your life. It is that ball of tension in your stomach that just won't go away, regardless of how much you attempt to put the project out of your mind and concentrate on fun activities. The feeling that we aren't accomplishing what we're supposed to accomplish is a terrible weight that can only be dismissed by actually finishing our work. It seems simple, yet so many of us live with that stress every day just so we can spend a bit more time procrastinating.

The medical effects of stress are also well-known, and present us with a laundry list of future problems. While eliminating your procrastination will help you feel better emotionally, it will also mitigate the onset of these health issues, potentially lengthening your life and allowing you to live more fully. You don't always have to feel off-balance. By simply eliminating your procrastination and getting rid of your stress, you'll become more in-tune with your world and feel more at peace.

This type of stress can also be harmful to those around you. It is likely to make you feel more on-edge, more distracted and less available during crunch time. You're more likely to snap at someone or even neglect them. While stress will certainly hurt you physically, it will also harm your relationships with the people that you care about.

This eventually becomes a cycle that's hard to break. You procrastinate, so then you neglect the ones you love. The next time around, fearing a repeat, you spend even more time with your loved ones while procrastinating your big project. Then, at the end, you're forced to scramble in order to get everything done on time. This type of relationship pattern is unhealthy for everyone involved, and only eliminating your procrastination can help you get out of it.

Procrastination isn't just stressful, however. It also leaves you feeling less fulfilled. Whatever you hope to accomplish, whether it is a small tasks or maybe it's one of your lifelong goals, the longer it takes you to finish the work, the more frustrated will you become. Accomplishing that task, as we've gone over, is highly fulfilling. You'll feel liberated, you'll feel productive, and you'll feel like you've done something meaningful.

If that's how you feel when you finish, it's easy to extrapolate how you feel when you *don't* finish: dissatisfied, unfulfilled, unproductive, like you're just wasting days. It's a simple decision to make. Unfortunately, most people don't see it as a decision. You *choose* to live a fulfilled life. You *choose* to accomplish your goals. You *choose* to stop procrastinating. You *choose* to embrace a healthier emotional state.

The only thing holding you back is your own bad habits. Fortunately, we can eliminate that.

Get Your FREE 40 Minute Tapping Session: http://velocityhousepresents.com/stop-procrastinating

Chapter 3

Elimination

So if we all know that procrastination is a terrible habit, why do we do it week after week, year after year? Every time we finish a project after too much procrastination, we say something along the lines of, "never again." How does, "never again," turn into, "I'll do it tomorrow," without even a moment's hesitation? How does anyone become a habitual "do-it-tomorrow" person?

A 2007 study by Gregory Schraw, Theresa Wadkins, and Lori Olafson said one key aspect of procrastination is that it's needless, and that's certainly true in retrospect. With hindsight, we can see that life would've been a lot easier if we simply would have finished our tasks at a reasonable pace instead of rushing to complete them right before the deadline.

Yet, if procrastination were really so "needless," it wouldn't be such a widespread epidemic. Our brain clearly recognizes some benefit to procrastination, or else we'd simply dismiss the idea and get on with our work. After all, we know what the reward is for finishing our work. The perceived "reward" we get for procrastinating must seem appealing enough to outweigh what we get for productivity.

When it comes to getting rid of procrastination, however, everything gets a lot more complicated.

In order to eliminate procrastination, we need to take the time and identify that procrastination will not help us. We need to stop procrastinating before we even start.

In order to do so, we need to figure out what that "reward" is. What does our brain see in procrastination that causes us to consistently keep doing it? What does our brain like about procrastination?

There is essentially no good reason to procrastinate. Procrastination will never help you. You won't be happy that you never finished such-and-such task, especially years down the line. It will continue to eat away at you until you either finish it or until it's too late to do anything about it. The only thing that procrastination can really cause is regret, both now and in the future.

No, there are no good reasons to procrastinate. Instead, there are only reasons that we think are good. We have excuses, in other words, that are just tenable enough to keep us from our work, even though we should know better. Excuses that lift the blame for any negative results.

The key to conquering procrastination is finding out what problem your procrastination solves. And the key to finding this out is "Questions." Ask yourself a few questions to determine this. Why do I keep procrastinating? What problem does procrastination solve for me? These can be broken down into two sub-questions: What is the 'downside' to finishing my project? What is the 'upside' to procrastination?

By answering these two sub-questions, we will be well on the way to eliminating your procrastination. In fact, answering these questions is essential to clearing out your bad work habits. Only by figuring out what procrastination is "solving," can you address the core of the problem.

Ask yourself: What is the 'downside' to finishing your project?

For instance, you may consciously assert that finishing your project is a great thing. Finally, that novel, drawing, design or website will be completed and your goal achieved. We're loath to believe that this could ever be a bad thing, because it's something we deeply desire to finish. Still, what are the downsides? What could go wrong? What is it that you fear, that's holding back?

Get Your FREE 40 Minute Tapping Session: http://velocityhousepresents.com/stop-procrastinating

On a superficial level, I'm sure you believe that you're excited to work on your project. Subconsciously, however, your brain sees some danger in that prospect. Your brain is attempting to sabotage your ambitions, through procrastination, thereby ensuring that your project is never actually completed.

Conversely, you must ask yourself, "What is the upside to procrastinating?"

When is the last time you did something that you didn't want to do, without being forced in some way? Even though you may consciously be against procrastination or feel ashamed by your bad habits, you continue the practice, because you think you need it. Maybe you need it as a shield from people's jealousy or rejection. Your brain thinks that procrastination is a good thing, or else it would stop.

Even though you know the huge downsides to procrastinating, your brain keeps putting you in that situation. It keeps convincing you to put off your work until the last minute and then to rush through everything.

The question is "Why?"

Are you helping yourself in any way? It certainly doesn't feel like procrastination is helpful the night before your deadline, and you're certain that everything is going to fall apart. You're always certain that *this* will be the time that you fail to finish.

It certainly doesn't feel like procrastination is helpful when you receive a bad mark on your paper, or your boss chastises you for turning in sub-par work that was clearly rushed, even though you had weeks to finish.

It certainly doesn't feel like procrastination is helping when you're forced to miss out on fun events because you put your work off for too long, and now you have to play catch-up solely due to your poor time management.

It certainly doesn't feel like procrastination is helping, even when your "work" is something as mundane as paying the bills, exercising, or taking out the trash. Suddenly it's Sunday, your day to relax, and you have to spend the entire day making up for the chores you didn't do all week. How many times has your "day off" turned into the day for doing

Get Your FREE 40 Minute Tapping Session: http://velocityhousepresents.com/stop-procrastinating

the dishes, cleaning the bathroom, mowing the lawn, taking out the trash and doing the laundry? Then your lack of a real day to relax makes you procrastinate even more during the week, as you try to snag some time from your busy schedule to entertain yourself.

And yet your brain keeps procrastinating. You rush through every project right before the deadline, even though you know that it's silly. You pile your dishes in the sink after dinner, sometimes for days on end. You don't update your resume, because then nobody can reject it. What's the problem? Where is the disconnect between what you want from your work habits, and what your brain is actually letting you accomplish?

The answers to these two questions, "What is the 'downside' of finishing the project?" and "What is the 'upside' to procrastinating?" are at the root of your issue. Answering each of them is the first step towards living a happier, more productive life.

The rest? Well, there is a way to help clear those mental roadblocks once we've identified them and eliminated their power over you. We'll go over that later in the book. For now, keep reading, and we'll go over how to zero in on the cause of your personal procrastination woes.

Chapter 4

Why Procrastinate?

Identifying the cause of our procrastination is the first step in eliminating it completely. Once we stop that perceived reward from having any power over us, procrastination instantly becomes less appealing. Though humans are very complex, we have a tendency to go for whatever option provides the most pleasure. Make procrastination less enticing, and you'll be amazed at how quickly you accomplish your work.

There are essentially four reasons why we procrastinate. At the root of each of these is a basic human need: safety. Procrastination keeps us safe in some way; it protects us from an outcome we fear. It takes no effort. It takes no special skill. It takes no conscious thought. It is a status quo arising from inactivity. When we procrastinate, we don't have to do anything, really, except exist.

Defeating procrastination, in every case, means stepping outside of this comfort zone. It's up to you to figure out what procrastination is keeping you safe from, and act accordingly.

1. Project Not "Ripe" Yet

If you've yet to begin working, there's a possibility that you're procrastinating simply because the project isn't ready to come out yet. You may think that you're ready to start, but your brain knows otherwise.

Your idea may be underdeveloped, and the project cannot move forward until you let it gestate a bit more. Maybe you even start to work on it, only to find that you lack the motivation or inspiration. You can't line up the energy.

Writer's block, for instance, could be caused by an idea that is only partially formed. It's safe to say that every writer experiences this at some point in their career, and it's a tough obstacle to get past. It's possible, however, that your brain is simply protecting you from starting a project before all your thoughts are lined up.

That's a small comfort when you're working against a deadline, but it's definitely a possibility.

While not all ideas spring from your brain fully-formed, your brain does *like* to have everything worked out ahead of time. In fact, some researchers have argued that this tendency or bias towards fully-formed ideas is not procrastination at all.

Robert Biswas-Diener, university professor and author of *Positive Psychology Coaching,* claims that some people who need fully-formed ideas in order to work are "incubators" instead of procrastinators.

Biswas-Diener describes a student, Mark, who seemed to be suffering from chronic procrastination. Mark simply could not find motivation without an impending deadline; he would spend days downloading music or browsing the Internet. Once the deadline was imminent, however, all the work would get completed in record time and with aplomb. Biswas-Diener theorized that Mark was not actually procrastinating at all, but incubating.

Incubators are the miracle workers we talked about earlier. They are only motivated when a deadline gets close, and they tend to do all their work at the last minute, yet they consistently turn out high-quality work under these rushed circumstances. Biswas-Diener argues that incubators aren't actually procrastinating, as much as they are turning ideas over in their minds and working everything out ahead of time. Then, when it comes time to put pen to paper, the words (or whatever else the project may consist of) are already there. The work is already done in their heads; they just need to record it.

While it's a great theory, and this type of person definitely seems to exist, it's still an unhealthy way to work. I find that these incubators tend to get just as stressed about their inactivity as regular procrastinators, and their health can suffer accordingly. Furthermore, they will also experience the same loss of freedom that we talked about earlier. As the deadline gets closer, incubators will find they have less and less time to spare. If anything goes wrong or there's a wrench in their plans, suddenly their typical process will fall apart.

Additionally, working with an incubator can be frustrating because they still *seem* like procrastinators. Just like a procrastinator, it seems like the incubator is never working until the last minute, causing their work to appear rushed or incomplete, even if it is of a high quality. An incubator might find that managers or clients label them as a procrastinator, even when the label isn't fair. While the incubator produces great work, it's better for everyone involved if the procrastination/incubation is eliminated from the outset.

The other problem, of course, is that too many people might identify themselves as incubators, even if the label doesn't fit. Procrastination has such a negative stigma, right? Being labeled a procrastinator is disheartening, or feels shameful. Being able to say that your procrastination serves a valuable purpose-that you're actually "incubating" and you shouldn't worry-seems great on the surface.

It can be hard to self-evaluate and decide whether you're actually an incubator or if you're simply justifying your procrastination. It's better to acknowledge procrastination in any form, whether incubation or not, is detrimental to your overall standard of living and should be eliminated so you can get on with your work in a timely fashion.

2. Fear of Failure

How often have you put off a project because you're afraid the end product won't turn out as good as you imagined? How often have you failed to finish something because you were afraid people would judge you harshly or criticize the result of your endless hours of work? Our brain wants to protect us from failure. We strive to keep our self-esteem intact. Failing at our aspirations or having someone else deem us failures can be incredibly damaging. That is how our brain perceives it, anyway. This form of procrastination is exceedingly common and paralyzing.

You can see it in the student who doesn't write a term paper. He would rather get an incomplete than deal with the ramifications of a bad grade. Would a bad grade mean that he isn't as good at writing as he thinks he is?

You can see it in the woman who always wanted to write the great American novel but has made dozens of false starts, or perhaps hasn't even begun the work. She fears her writing, her life's work, will never be read by anyone, and she will never reach the level of fame for which she aspires. She may fear that the book would receive bad reviews or become a laughingstock.

You can see it in the man who plays guitar for twenty years in his bedroom but never tried to start a band or write any songs, even though it was his biggest aspiration. What if his songs sounded worse in real life than they did in his head? How could he keep his sense of self intact if people rejected his work and scoffed at his lyrics?

Though these are all artistic examples, this fear of failure can cause inactivity in all aspects of your life. For instance, you may procrastinate going to the doctor for weeks on end, simply because you're afraid of what you might hear. Even though the doctor is only there to help, you fear hearing that you haven't taken care of your body. You fear being judged by the doctor. It feels like a personal failure.

This fear of failure can keep you from living a happy and fulfilled life. It can prevent you from pursuing your dreams, instead relegating you to a life spent accepting the average and wasting your potential. This an extremely damaging form of procrastination, because it causes you to withdraw. It also ignores the fact that the only way you'll get better is through practice. You might not create your masterpiece on your first try, but that's not to say that you won't create a master piece further down the line. Talent will only get you part of the way there. Practice is key to improving, and you can't practice if you aren't willing to make mistakes.

The adage, "you'll never know until you try," applies here. You really never will know your true potential until you put yourself out there. Your brain wants to keep you safe, but you need to overrule that instinct and endanger your self-esteem in order to test your mettle. Safety is overrated.

This fear of failure affects all people, even the masters. Regardless of how well-regarded someone is within their industry, eventually they will produce a lemon. If someone experiences success, they're even more likely to fear failure the next time around. If they release a poor product, they're bound to get criticism on all fronts. Hearing: "Washed up," or "not the same as the old days," are common nightmares. Some will even wonder if they're really as good as people think, or if it was just a fluke the first time around. This is sometimes known informally as Impostor Syndrome or the Impostor Phenomenon, and it can bring a great career to a halt.

Unfortunately, the people who are most at risk here are the perfectionists among us. While the woman in my earlier example didn't want to write her novel because she feared it wouldn't be accepted or that she'd be criticized by others, the perfectionist only fears the inability to live up to his or her own demands. Perfectionists procrastinate because they are convinced their own work will never be good enough to meet their own exacting standards. They criticize *themselves.* They fear failing *themselves* instead of failing some unknown audience.

This goes close in hand with people who are convinced that they are already failures. They don't even give themselves a chance, because they just know their work is inadequate, even though they've never given it a try. This is an identity issue, and it stems from a poor self-esteem. In this case, the person's confidence is already so low that it prevents him or her from taking any risks. It's possible that this person was already judged as inadequate in some other way and now projects that feeling onto a new field of interest. He or she will ruin

Get Your FREE 40 Minute Tapping Session: *http://velocityhousepresents.com/stop-procrastinating*

any opportunity to move ahead, convinced that it won't feel right or will only end in tragedy.

Whatever the case, a fear of failure can be crippling. I've worked with numerous clients who procrastinate solely because they fear failure, judgment or criticism, even if it's not a conscious thought. Conquering fear is always a challenging task, but doing so is always incredibly satisfying.

3. Fear of Success

While fear of failure is widely acknowledged in our society, its counterpart is all but ignored. Fear of success can be just as intimidating or paralyzing as fear of failure, and is more common than people realize.

In this case, the brain is keeping you safe by attempting not to "rock the boat." You're afraid to shine, and your procrastination stems from a desire to not stand out, to hold back or appear ordinary, so you sabotage your efforts in hopes of laying low. You embrace the average. You normalize your own output, conforming to whatever standard you imagine is most liked by your community. Your brain is procrastinating so that you don't becomes special or stand out. In other words, you fear how success will upset your day-to-day life and how it will cause others to perceive you. You're afraid to be the beacon on the hill. You're set against becoming the top dog. You've got a good thing going already, and you don't want to upset the balance.

For instance, what if your business explodes right out of the gate, and you become immensely successful? Will your friends still treat you the same, even though they know of your success? What about your friend who has been trying to start his or her own business, but is failing? How will you face them, knowing that you accomplished easily what they have yet to accomplish?

If your business succeeds and is catapulted into the spotlight, you may attract unwanted negative attention. People may call you greedy, or they may say that you never "deserved" the success that you've achieved. Others may be jealous of your success and will say nasty things behind your back (or to your face). How will you deal with this change in circumstance?

I've worked with many clients that intentionally sabotaged their work so they wouldn't stand out.

They hid their talent, afraid to really stand out because they worried they'd look "too" good. They didn't want to upset their business partner, their colleagues, their family, their jealous sister, or any combination of these people. If their ideas succeeded, they feared it would cause others to look down on them for their "luck," even if the process involved had nothing to do with luck but a lot of hard work.

Others I've worked with torpedoed their careers because they felt greedy. They already made so much money or had such abundance, that they felt wrong making any more. Even though they might deserve more for their high-quality work, the guilt was overwhelming to them. Procrastination prevented them from advancing any further, so that they never had to worry about getting a raise or being promoted.

These are the kinds of fears that your brain dreams up that promote inactivity or procrastination. The problem, of course, is that these fears are really only holding you back. Eventually you have to go after your own happiness instead of worrying about what others think. If your friend is going to be jealous of your success, then he or she was not a true friend to begin with. A true friend will be happy that you are achieving your goals, happy that you are enjoying your work and feeling productive.

You're going to have to rock the boat. You might make some enemies or lose a few friends in the process, but you'll never be happy if you constantly are asking "what if?" The brain may fear change, but it's just a part of life.

You deserve to achieve success, because you've put in the hard work to do so. Don't intentionally handicap yourself, procrastinating to squander your potential, out of some misguided attempt to protect yourself. You've worked hard to accomplish your goals. Now you simply have to let yourself finish the job.

4. Rebellion

Let's face it: rules are a pain. Deadlines are even worse. If you're someone who's sick of working for "the man" or tired of being treated like the proverbial cog in the machine, it's possible that you're procrastinating out of rebellion.

Does this sound familiar? Your boss is always handing you projects that need to be done as soon as possible. You're a dutiful worker for months, or even years, but eventually the grind gets to you. You're tired of working under a deadline for a boss that doesn't appreciate you, so you finally resolve to intentionally miss the next deadline.

You purposefully fail to meet even the easiest deadlines, trying to assert control over your life in some small way. You become passive-aggressive in your work. You insist on doing everything your way, instead of following standard procedures.

Your interaction with your boss deteriorates. What was once a respectful working relationship becomes a series of small confrontations and slights. Things seem to fall apart for you at work, and your career suffers as a result. You find that you have trouble following rules of any kind, even if they're innately reasonable. You long for the day when you can strike out on your own and work for yourself.

In order to get back at rules or deadlines, you may find yourself constantly taking shortcuts. After all, why should you do your best work if no one will notice the difference? It's not like you need to do your best work at this job, anyway; you don't plan to work there long term.

You may resent anyone looking over your shoulder, whether at work or in your personal life. A father, boss, or partner who keeps you "in-check" may rub you the wrong way, even if the person means well. This attitude may infest everything you do. You may continually procrastinate cleaning the closet or the bathroom, because it feels like a "should" to you, and you hate anything that feels like a "should." You're perpetually ready to start exercising "tomorrow." That great diet you saw can also wait. You want to live your life in your own way, and damn the consequences.

This form of procrastination is the most damaging, and it must be addressed immediately. Not only are you harming your productivity, but you are destroying your personal and work relationships. In this case, the procrastination is actually the least of your worries. It's just a symptom of a greater issue that needs to be taken care of. Failure to address the root issue can be catastrophic and can cause irreparable damage.

By eliminating this form of procrastination, you will enhance not only your productivity, but all aspects of your life. We can get your career back on track, mend your personal relationships, and get you back on a path to achieve your aspirations again.

As we've established, everyone procrastinates for a different reason. Identifying the root of your personal procrastination habit is the first step towards eliminating the problem. This is the hard part; it's the part that most of my clients struggle with most, because it's difficult to do an unbiased self-evaluation. Many times, my clients will identify a root cause of their procrastination that ends up being just one of numerous causes. Often, that initial identified cause is only a minor factor, and there is something much deeper that is contributing to their procrastination habit. That's completely normal.

The key is to identify a starting point. Figure out something that you can use as your starting point. Inevitably, you'll come up with other reasons for your procrastination as everything moves forward. You can integrate those as they arise. Don't worry about finding the deepest, subconscious origins of your procrastination from the get-go. They'll come out eventually.

In spite of how pervasive procrastination is in our culture, it does not have to be a fact of life. In fact, procrastination is one of our habits that we can eliminate most easilyonce we've identified the cause. Provided you use the correct methods, you can increase your productivity and develop good work habits almost immediately.

Now that we've identified the cause of your procrastination, it's finally time to eliminate it.

Chapter 5

Introduction to Meridian Tapping

I thought I had everything worked out.

I thought I had worked out how to be an adult.

I went to school, training to be a clinical social worker. I was going to help people sort through their mental health issues. Finding the work invigorating, I resolved to increase my expertise. I continued on with my education, eventually earning a doctorate in Clinical Hypnotherapy. If I was going to help people, I was certainly going to make sure I was giving them the best help possible.

Yet, not long after I earned my doctoral degree, I felt things had stagnated. For years I had been fighting a pitched battle against procrastination, and each year, I gave a bit more ground. I was plagued with all four of the types of procrastination listed in the last chapter. I was afraid of being criticized and my work rejected; I was afraid to shine; I was tired of deadlines, and my procrastination made it impossible for me to come up with any ideas, even if I wanted to work on them.

In a moment of realization, I saw that I had made the same income for the last two years. I had failed to increase my earnings even a little bit. I was in that most dangerous of spells: a rut.

What's worse, I knew I had more to offer.

In 1997, I started looking for ways to expand the tools I used to help others. I felt compelled to broaden my horizons and take on new challenges.

The result? I began learning "tapping" therapies from Dr. Fred Gallo, a psychologist who had once studied with Dr. Roger Callahan. Dr. Callahan was the founder of an entire field known as TFT, or Thought Field Therapy, where the "tapping" method was originally created.

Shortly thereafter, I learned about the work of Gary Craig, founder of a complementary program known as EFT, or Emotional Freedom Techniques. I began working extensively with Craig, and began a lifelong journey of fully understanding and utilizing his methods. EFT also used the tapping that I'd been studying with Dr. Gallo, and EFT is the program that I now use exclusively with clients. Eventually, I was even designated one of the first EFT Masters in the world. It's a program that I know works, because I've seen it work wonders for countless clients. It's the best program I've found for helping my clients literally transform their lives. It also improved my life dramatically.

So what is EFT? What is tapping?

This is what we are going to use to eliminate your procrastination. Exciting, am I right? We're going to get really in-depth in the next chapter, especially in terms of how tapping can eliminate your procrastination, but for now, I'm just going to give you a general overview of the technique and its history. Forgive me if you've read one of my other books, or if you've already worked with tapping in your personal life, since a lot of this background information might be common knowledge to you. We'll get to applications of tapping to eliminate procrastination soon enough, I promise.

The easiest way for me to describe the meridian tapping technique, if you're unfamiliar with the concept, is "emotional acupuncture." Basic concepts are the same as those in acupuncture, despite the fact that we don't need needles to accomplish the same goals. If you've ever studied or tried acupuncture, you'll probably recognize term "meridian." If not, let me explain it to you.

The meridians are ancient concepts, originating in China over four-thousand years ago. The meridians are channels that carry energy throughout the human body. Unblocked (or clear) meridians ensure that the body is kept in balance at all times, promoting a healthy body and mind.

These are the channels through which flows our "chi," or life-energy. An unfettered or clean flow of chi energy is absolutely essential to a healthy human body, and meridians are essential in the process. Think of the meridians as arteries and veins, and rather than carrying your blood, they transport your chi energy.

Just as a blockage in one of your blood vessels can cause long-term health problems, so can a hindrance in one of your meridians. A disruption in the flow of your chi energy can throw your body out of balance, harm your health and cause severe stress and bad habits.

Acupuncture is designed to fix the flow of chi in the body, correcting any imbalances and repairing problems that resulted from disrupted chi. Yet acupuncture is an incredibly complex art and requires years of study. There are potentially hundreds of acupuncture points throughout the body.

Tapping, especially in the Emotional Freedom Techniques tradition, relies on the basic tenets of acupuncture but expands the focus. The tapping technique still firmly focuses on the belief that mental, emotional and physical health relies on a clear flow of chi through the meridians. All of your problems in life result from a blockage of one kind or another, and rectifying that blockage is vital in fixing whatever problem you're experiencing. As the name "meridian tapping" indicates, we'll be focusing our efforts on these meridians.

The difference, however, is that tapping is easy, even for a novice. It's quick; it's painless, and it works. Tapping is an elegant solution for people from all walks of life. It works just as well for the businessman or engineer as it does for the musician or writer, because fundamentally, we're all the same. All of us have meridian points to tap into, and all of us need to regularly examine ourselves and keep a healthy flow of chi in order to reach our maximum potential.

Get Your FREE 40 Minute Tapping Session: http://velocityhousepresents.com/stop-procrastinating

I've yet to meet a willing client for which tapping did not produce immediate, observable results in their personal and professional lives. It's the perfect technique. Better still, it is much easier than comparable programs.

In EFT tapping, we focus on nine meridian points. Additionally, I'm going to teach you how to tap efficiently, how hard to tap, and what statements you should use at each tapping point to attain maximum results. That's coming up in later chapters, but it's something for you to look forward to.

By the time you're done with this book, you'll be able to use tapping to solve all sorts of problems in your life, not just your procrastination.

While the physical act of tapping on the meridian points is crucial to recreate the healthy flow of chi, I also incorporate another key philosophy vital to your success.

It's called the "Law of Attraction."

Again, just like tapping, we'll be practicing the concept in more detail within the next chapter. I know there are a lot of concepts in this chapter with which you may be unfamiliar with, or may only have a passing knowledge of. I want to reiterate one more time that it's okay. By the end of this book, I guarantee that you'll feel entirely comfortable with these ideas and will be able to fully utilize the EFT tapping technique. This chapter is simply here to provide you with background knowledge on some of these concepts before we begin using them and exploring them in greater detail.

If you've ever read the book *The Secret* (or seen the film adaptation), you have at least some understanding of the Law of Attraction. The Law of Attraction is a principle summed up most elegantly by William Walker Atkinson in 1906: "like attracts like." If that sounds a bit too evasive, let me elaborate. The Law of Attraction is centered on the belief that by focusing on positive thoughts, we attract positivity into our lives. Naturally, the converse negative thoughts will attract negative results.

One of my favorite authors on this subject, Annie Besant, is also one of the originators of the concept. Besant wrote that the Law of Attraction functions similarly to the law of gravity. Instead of focusing on mass or the realm of the physical world, however, the Law of Attraction focuses on your vibration and your mood. Positive thinking will raise your vibration and attract the change you want to see in yourself.

Using the Law of Attraction, you can change your entire life. Dispel all those negative thoughts, and learn to bring positivity into your life. *Allow* feelings of gratitude, optimism, joy and hope into your life, and see how big of a difference that it makes.

I'm a huge proponent of the Law of Attraction and have used its principles to help numerous clients with my "Attracting Abundance" program. It's the second half of the formula. It's the jelly to EFT's peanut butter. They are the age-old peas in the pod. In fact, they complement each other so well that it's hard for me to imagine using one without the other. While the Law of Attraction is certainly powerful on its own, linking it with EFT tapping creates something far more compelling. Something that can affect more change with less effort on your part. By combining the two techniques, it's never been easier to bring about positive change in your life.

Here's how it works. There are two main components to achieve success in this program. We want to lower our resistance. Resistance is defined as our negative feelings: guilt, fear, anxiety and resentment, to name a few. EFT tapping focuses on this aspect. It helps us release our negative feelings and fears.

The other half of the recipe is raising our vibration. Our vibration is defined simply as our mood. Actively raising our vibration leaves us more open to observing the abundance in our lives or feeling better in general. It comes from a place of gratitude and appreciation.

The Law of Attraction is a philosophy that focuses on speeding up this vibration. For example, someone who is genuinely expressing gratitude daily and notices when things go well has a higher "vibration" than someone who focuses on the pessimistic angle. Maintaining a positive outlook can be challenging, what with how stressful life can be sometimes.

Thus, EFT and the Law of Attraction are best used together. EFT will dispel our negative feelings and let us eradicate anything in the way of our positivity and gratitude. Releasing our fears and anxieties makes feeling grateful easier and more natural, allowing the Law of Attraction to do its work and amplify our optimistic outlook. The two are a natural complement.

Why wouldn't you use every tool available to you in the struggle against procrastination? If you were building a house-and you weren't procrastinating on that task, of course-would you leave your hammer unused at the bottom of a toolbox? Of course not. You'd pull out anything that could help you. The same is true for this. Combining the Law of Attraction with theEFT tapping technique, as you'll see in the next chapter, will have you making breakthroughs and observing incredible results within just a few short sessions, doubling your effectiveness.

How do I know that this combination works?

Remember the opening of this chapter, and that dismayed woman (yours truly) who couldn't seem to bring abundance into her own life? Combining the Law of Attraction and EFT tapping is what got me out of that rut and into a place of attracting substantial abundance.

Using the same principles I'm teaching you in this book, I managed to get rid of my own hang-ups and roadblocks. I stopped limiting myself. Prior to my use of these techniques, I was the poster child of someone who prevented their own success. I created my own obstacles. I had some worries that I now know are very common:

"It's impossible to earn a lot of money in my business." "I'm afraid to shine and stand out." "It's not safe to be successful."

These thoughts were stumbling blocks that were single-handedly preventing me from moving forward in my career at the time. Using EFT tapping, I cleared those worries from my mind. I erased their hold over me.

I no longer worried that it wasn't safe to be successful or about standing out in my field. I no longer stressed about what I was earning, or that it was impossible for me to earn more. Rather, I knew the exact opposite was true. I recognized that I was only holding myself back, and that I had finally found the way forward. I understood that I could attract abundance and my desires. I saw my circumstances change on a daily basis, my life improving in leaps and bounds.

The results were magnificent. Better than I ever could have dreamed prior to studying EFT and including those concepts in my own lifestyle. I quickly increased my income by over seven-hundred percent and greatly broadened the coaching help and advice I was able to provide my clients.

I applied the same principles to other aspects of my life, improving just as much. I eliminated my chronic, long-term problem with insomnia. I released grief issues that had gone unresolved for far too long. I completely eradicated my cravings for cigarettes and severely curtailed my food cravings. I relieved chronic pains.

I also eliminated a long-term procrastination problem. The war is over. I won. That's why I'm so excited to write this book: tapping works!

The truth is, I barely even recognize that scared, sabotaging woman from before.

Since that time, I've reached a point in my career that is both invigorating and enjoyable. I've also helped countless clients around the world move past their own personal stumbling blocks, including smoking, weight loss problems, childhood and adult traumas (PTSD), pain, stress, insomnia, success and abundance, and career self-sabotage.

We're going to do the same with your procrastination. When we're done, the reasons that you've been procrastinating all this time should seem trivial. I've had clients say, "Why should I care about those things that were holding me back? They don't affect me." Those clients were right. All of those things that seem so powerful, those things that make your brain think that procrastination is actually *saving* you from something, will become meaningless. You can recognize them as the excuses they are, so that you can get on with living. Doesn't that sound nice? Refreshing? Liberating, even? Take away the reward of procrastination,

Get Your FREE 40 Minute Tapping Session: *http://velocityhousepresents.com/stop-procrastinating*

and it suddenly looks like a really silly idea to your brain. Good riddance, procrastination!

Without a doubt, the primary thing holding you back from your true potential is *yourself*. Change yourself, change your attitude, and we can eliminate this stubborn procrastination. Let's get rid of those excuses. No more stress about deadlines; no more stress about unfinished projects; no more stress in general. We're going to turn your productivity around, and we're going to do so in record time.

All I need is your cooperation and your willingness to think positively. Are you ready to learn the "secret" to successfully eliminating procrastination? Are you ready to learn how to tap your way to productivity?

Then, let's get started.

Chapter 6

An in-Depth Look at EFT

How long have you lived with procrastination? How long has it been holding you back from your full potential, causing you stress in both your work and home relationships and keeping you from absolute fulfillment?

It doesn't matter what you answer. Whether it's one day, one year, a decade, or your entire life-any amount of time is too long.

It doesn't have to be that way. What could you do with just one more useful, productive hour per day? In these next few chapters I'm going to give you all the tools to make it so. Don't struggle with procrastination ever again. Simply follow my directions to a healthier, happier lifestyle. It's as easy as that.

One of my favorite aspects of EFT is that it's so easy for people to learn. While not everyone is going to become an EFT expert overnight, it is entirely possible for you to start seeing clear and observable changes in your life, even when you're just beginning.

As if that weren't enough, the EFT technique has applications outside of eliminating procrastination. While this bad habit is the particular foible we're focusing on in this book, keep in mind that it's not the only bad habit you can eliminate with proper use of meridian tapping.

Other programs I've experimented with are simply not as effective as EFT or take so long to become effective that the patient loses hope.

Get Your FREE 40 Minute Tapping Session: *http://velocityhousepresents.com/stop-procrastinating*

Sustaining results from my program will take some work and time on your part, and you're going to want to keep practicing EFT in order to achieve stronger results, but I can guarantee that you'll be amazed at the difference my program can make in a short amount of time.

EFT is simple for anyone to remember. It consists of nine meridian points, tapping, and then we add the Law of Attraction. This is all you'll need to learn in order to get started. When I put it that way, it doesn't seem very intimidating at all, does it?

We are now going to combine all the work we've done to this point, everything we've learned, as we move onto the last steps. It's the foundational knowledge that you need in order to use EFT effectively.

The only thing that we're missing now is technique: the physicality, the motions. You know all about what EFT and tapping can do. Now, how do you do it? There are four basic parts of EFT, and it's very simple to grasp the technique if you use all the components properly.

Step One: Choosing A Target

This one is exceptionally easy for you, because we've already done this in some small measure. You see, our first step is to decide what we are aiming our tapping at. It's what we're going to focus all of our positive energy on as we move into the other steps. If you purchased this book, it's likely that you already have a target in mind: your procrastination habits.

Still, I think we can add a bit more nuance to your target. While it's all well and good to focus on your procrastination, and that's a fine beginning if you can't think of anything else, it's a pretty huge target if taken all at once. There may be dozens of reasons for your procrastination, and it's much more effective to target them one at a time rather than targeting procrastination on a general level.

Additionally, this information will be useful if you ever decide to expand your usage of EFT into other aspects of your life. After all, my hope is that you'll be so impressed with your procrastination results that you'll use tapping to help with any number of stumbling blocks in your life. I firmly believe in the power of this program, and I know it can help others like it's helped me.

You see, the largest problem with using "procrastination" as a target is that it's a very nebulous concept. The key to EFT is right in the name-*emotion.* What kind of emotion accompanies procrastination?

It's likely that procrastination conjures up negative emotions in you: stress, anger or despair. These emotions, however, are results of our procrastination, not causes. It's akin to treating the symptoms of a condition instead of the root of the issue. It doesn't work well when we're treating a physical issue, and it doesn't work any better when rectifying our mental blocks.

My basic advice to people who are new to EFT is to choose an emotion, a symptom, or an event to focus on, but what we're really aiming for is relating everything back to emotion. The latter two are simply easier for people to think about or conceptualize. For instance, if you pick a symptom, try to understand what emotion is possibly related to that symptom. Why does that symptom relate to fear? If you pick an event to focus on, figure out what emotional residue-perhaps guilt, anxiety, or depression-stems from that event, fueling your negative feelings.

Don't worry, however, if you can't get a handle on all of this up front. It's entirely possible that you go into your first tapping session only recognizing "procrastination" as your target. It is, after all, our ultimate foe in this book. It's the dragon we must slay.

If you can't get to the root emotions yet, you will. The wonderful thing about EFT is that as we become more aware, and those root causes have a way of bubbling to the surface. Your mind will let you know what the problem is eventually, even if you can't think of it now.

Think way back to when I discussed why people commonly procrastinate. Remember our four categories? I procrastinate because my project isn't ripe yet, because I fear failure, because I fear success, or because I am rebelling against authority in my life. If you fit into any of those four categories, try using one of *those* as your starting point.

Get Your FREE 40 Minute Tapping Session: http://velocityhousepresents.com/stop-procrastinating

A fear of failure is far more emotionally resonant than "procrastination." Ultimately we want to eliminate our procrastination, but tapping just as easily eliminates your fear of failure: a concept attached to far more emotional distress. When someone says they have a fear of failure, you can feel that fear. You can understand that. Someone saying they procrastinate? That's much more nuanced and could spring from any number of causes.

As a bonus, eliminating your fear of failure will come with all sorts of pleasant side effects, above and beyond saying goodbye to procrastination. Suddenly, failure won't seem so bad or scary, and you'll be able to recognize failure as an opportunity to improve and advance further in your career. You'll divorce your failures from your self-esteem, treating them as learning experiences. You'll be more self-confident and determined. The difference this can have on your life is unfathomable.

Sounds a bit better than just targeting procrastination, right?

Be honest with yourself. Pick a target that will address your procrastination, but that will also have a personal emotional relevance, if at all possible. The attached emotion will come in handy during the next step.

Step Two: Rating

Before we start tapping, we need to quantify our feelings about the target so that later we can see if EFT is having any effect. To accomplish this, we use a simple zero-to-ten point scale, where zero is the least severe and ten is the most severe response possible.

Whatever you ended up choosing as a target, think of it right now. Really dig deep and focus on it.

How do you feel?

More importantly, how *much* do you feel?

It's safe to say we're getting rid of our hang-ups and stumbling blocks-negativity, in other words. Because of that, the key aspect of this rating system is "discomfort" or "distress," depending on how severe your reaction is.

This is where the emotional aspect comes into play. Even if your target is simply general procrastination, rather than something more focused, we still need to know the intensity of your emotional response in order to properly quantify our later results and ensure that we're making progress.

Rating is doubly important, because we don't want to waste our efforts on a target that points in the wrong direction. Rating before and after tapping allows us to recalibrate our target if necessary, sharpen it or redirect it, so that we can advance. We want to make sure we're focusing our efforts on the right thing to reduce stress and anxiety.

Try it again. Clear your mind of everything except your target and its accompanying emotional response. Prod at it, feel how much discomfort or distress this negative emotion causes you. Then numerically rate your response.

Don't worry about what other people would say. Don't rate your discomfort against some objective human discomfort. In other words, don't abstain from rating your discomfort as high just because someone else probably has it worse. If you feel like your procrastination is holding you back or is causing you a great amount of discomfort, that is absolutely valid. These numbers are all relative.

The goal here is to eventually reduce your discomfort to zero. That's when we know that its power over you has been broken. Don't worry if you don't get there in one session or if you never get to zero. There will be some problems that are so deeply rooted that you may never fully dispel them, at least not without help from someone I have trained or can refer you to for additional coaching.

We simply want measurable results. We want you to restore your function, and we want to bring those tens, eights, even sixes, down to the lower end of the spectrum-to zeros, ones, or even to threes. We want to decrease the target's power over you enough so that you can get

Get Your FREE 40 Minute Tapping Session: *http://velocityhousepresents.com/stop-procrastinating*

back to functioning properly. The same fears may come back and nag at you occasionally, but you'll now know how to confront it.

If your initial rating is too low, a one, two or three, I recommend choosing a different target.

Now, you're ready for the next step!

Step Three: The Set Up Statement

The setup statement is the most crucial aspect of EFT, and it relies on the information you came up with in the previous steps. It's also the part of EFT that will take the most practice.

The basic building blocks of the setup statement are twofold and have stayed the same since EFT was initially developed: name the problem and combine it with an affirmation of acceptance.

It looks something like this:

"Even though I have this problem, I deeply and profoundly love and accept myself, anyway."

The first half is where we name our problem, the second is where we affirm that we accept that flaw in ourselves and begin to eliminate the issue.

First of all, when creating your setup statement, you'll name the problem. Well, that's easy. We already identified the problem when we chose our target!

We want to combine our problem with a statement of acceptance, in order to begin the healing process; they tend to follow along the lines of, "I deeply and profoundly love and accept myself anyway," or "I deeply and profoundly accept who I am and how I feel," or "I appreciate every part of me."

The point is to acknowledge that you have an issue-whether it's procrastination or any other symptom, event or emotional concern, and then affirm that you accept yourself anyway, that you're okay with who you are.

Get Your FREE 40 Minute Tapping Session: *http://velocityhousepresents.com/stop-procrastinating*

Personally, this is what I find most beautiful about EFT. The setup statement is both incredibly powerful and poignant.

The most important thing to keep in mind is that your setup statement must be positive, affirming and accepting. This is the Law of Attraction at work. By ending our setup statements with positivity, we promote well-being and keep our minds and bodies in a healthy place. We allow ourselves to be healed, even as we admit what has been holding us back from that healing.

For instance, if you have a fear of failure, your setup statement may be:

"Even though I'm afraid that I'll be criticized, I deeply and profoundly accept who I am and how I feel."

Or

"Even though I don't want to leave my comfort zone, I choose to respect who I am and how I feel."

There's a lot of variation available, and it may take you a while to figure out what's most effective for your personal process. As you conduct your tapping sessions and become more comfortable with both yourself and EFT, you may find yourself further refining your setup statement. This is entirely natural.

Don't worry if you're feeling stuck. As I said at the start of this section, the setup statement requires practice and trial and error. The formula's simple surface is deceptive. There are hidden depths to crafting a setup statement, and it can be hard to nail down exactly what you need in order to best target your mental blocks.

With that in mind, I've provided a number of additional suggestions for your personal setup statements later on in the book. Feel free to look them over and adapt them into your own program. You may find that you're more comfortable with some than others. That's absolutely fine! Choose whichever statements that you think will get you to your goal.

Use the rating system as a guide for your statement's effectiveness. If your discomfort isn't decreasing or you're becoming more distressed, it's a sign that you should focus on a different target or craft a different setup statement. Just keep practicing!

Whatever you do, do not skip the setup statement! It's absolutely crucial to the program, as you will see when you embark on the next step: the actual, physical tapping.

Step Four: Tapping

Tapping is the heart of EFT. This "emotional acupuncture" is where the real healing begins. We've got our target; we've got our initial rating, and we've got our setup statement. Now it's time for us to physically tap on our meridian points and reset the flow of chi through the body. Soon enough, we'll clear out any blockages and have you feeling inspired.

Prior to beginning your tapping session, it is of utmost importance to make sure that you settle in a calm, comfortable area free of distractions, a place where you can remain absolutely focused on the target. While tapping is vital to the process, your own attention is just as important. These initial tapping sessions are bound to be the most intense, since you've never worked on eliminating this trait before. Later on, when you're performing preventative tapping or maintaining your productivity, you'll probably only need ten to fifteen minutes for an effective session. For now, however, plan to set aside 30 minutes or so to really dig deep with these problems. The more focused you remain throughout the session, the better your results will be.

Think of your brain as an enormous filing system for your thoughts and memories. When we go through a tapping session, we're looking to change one thing in particular about ourselves. I like to tell those new to EFT to call up the target as if they were opening up a file or a document on a computer. For instance, call up the file in your brain titled "procrastination." It will be full of reasons why you like procrastinating.

Tapping essentially edits these files. Focusing our brains allows us to keep the file open while the tapping reduces the fear or negative emotion. When we've completed a session, the file has usually been altered by reducing your fear and allowing more positive thoughts.

Get Your FREE 40 Minute Tapping Session: http://velocityhousepresents.com/stop-procrastinating

AN IN-DEPTH LOOK AT EFT | **45**

Does that make sense? If so, you can see why remaining focused on the target is essential. Otherwise, you will be going through the physical motions of meridian tapping and not getting the mental benefits. You may still get some general benefits, but it won't necessarily fix your targeted problem.

The actual tapping process is relatively easy. You simply have to focus on the emotion you want to reduce and allow more positive solutions into your life. In the next chapter, I will be including step-by-step guides for a number of different tapping exercises to help you through the process.

Diagram of Tapping Points

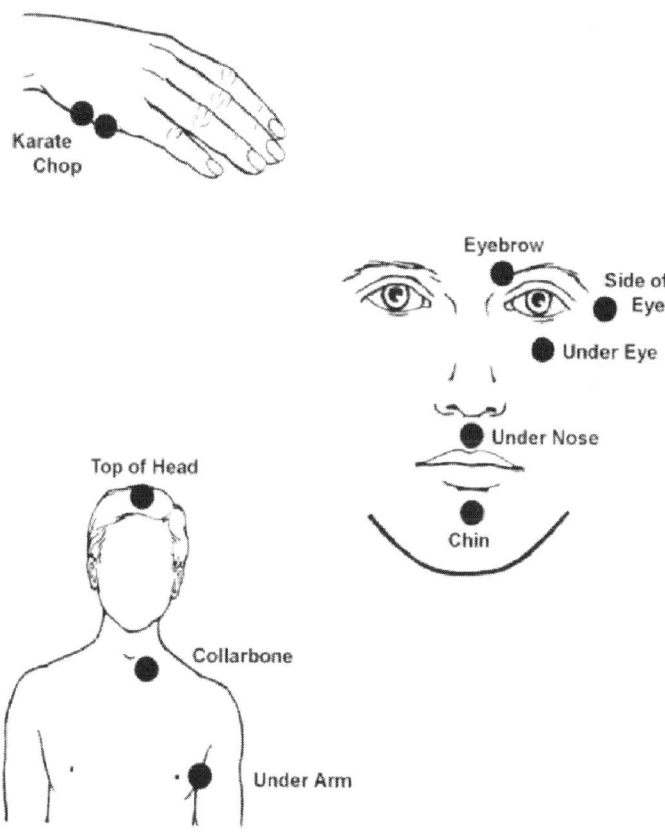

Get Your FREE 40 Minute Tapping Session: *http://velocityhousepresents.com/stop-procrastinating*

Start with the Karate Chop Point, which is between your pinky and your wrist on the outside of your hand. Picture the section of the hand that a Karate master would use to break through a board, the fleshy part on the outside edge; that's where we want to tap. It doesn't matter what hand you use; it's purely a matter of preference. I'm right-handed, so I tap with the fingers of my right hand onto the left edge of my left hand, but do whatever feels more comfortable.

The physical tapping is only half of the formula, however. I hope you've got your setup statement ready, because this is where we're going to use it.

As you tap on your Karate Chop Point, say your setup statement three times. For instance, if your setup statement is "even though I am afraid of failure, I deeply and profoundly love and accept myself anyway," you should repeat that whole phrase three times while tapping on the fleshy part of your hand.

The setup statement is like a primer for the EFT technique. It kick-starts our system to accept the work done by the tapping, allowing us to positively affect change in our lifestyle. It alerts our body and mind, telling it, "this is what we're working on in this session." It gives us focus and resolve.

That's why the setup statement is so crucial to EFT. Everything in a tapping session relies on the setup statement, because it focuses our energies on the target. A successful setup statement primes us for further changes and begins the healing process.

We do this each time we've chosen a target and devised a new setup statement.

Now, we tap on the sequence of acupuncture points included in the EFT treatment. For these points, we're going to tap with two fingers, at a moderate pace-faster than the seconds hand on the clock, but not so fast that you're rushing. Tap firmly, but not too hard. We're just trying to signal to our body to reset the flow of chi. The effectiveness of tapping comes from making contact with the point on your body. Don't hurt yourself!

Get Your FREE 40 Minute Tapping Session: *http://velocityhousepresents.com/stop-procrastinating*

As you tap, remember to stay focused on the problem. We want to make sure you're getting the most out of each session, and this requires your full attention.

In order to help with this, we will say a "reminder phrase" each time we tap on a new point. Name the problem. This will keep your brain focused on the task at hand. It will keep that file open and ready for you to edit.

The reminder phrase is similar to the setup statement, but involves only the first half-the problem. For instance, where the setup statement might say, "even though I am afraid of failure," the reminder phrase would say, "my fear of failure." It doesn't have to be the same each time. You might say, "my fear of failure," the first time and then say, "this fear of failure that causes me to procrastinate," the next time.

Just make sure you're encapsulating the problem, calling up the file, and reminding yourself of the target each time. This helps you tune in to the problem, letting you reduce stress and anxiety. The reminder phrase is essential to eliminating the discomfort or distress you feel about the target.

For sample reminder statements, feel free to peek at the next chapter, where I have provided plenty of examples.

Get Your FREE 40 Minute Tapping Session: *http://velocityhousepresents.com/stop-procrastinating*

Below is the Sequence of Points You Will Be Tapping on

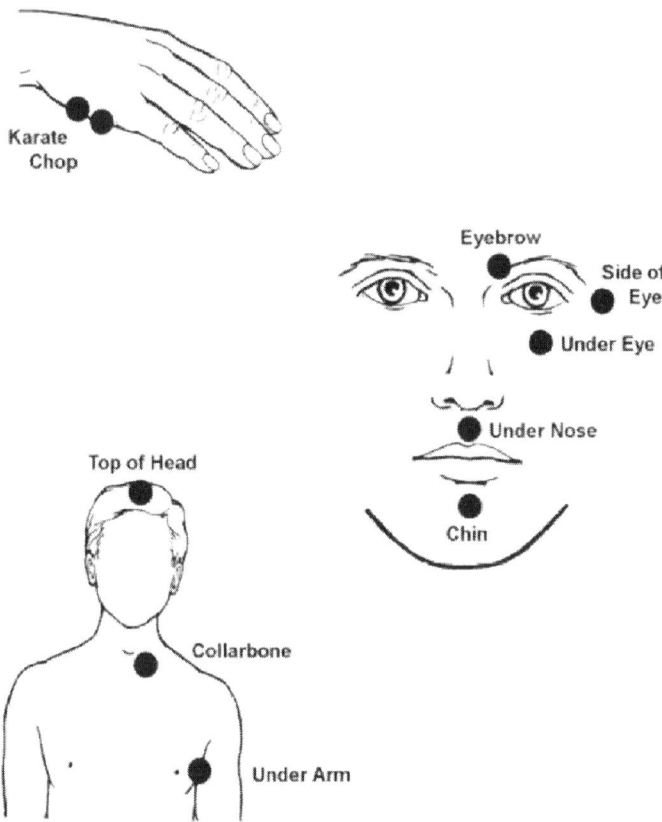

The first acupuncture point after the karate chop point is right above your nose, at the beginning of your eyebrow. It's not so high as to be in your third eye point; simply level with your eyebrow. As with the Karate Chop Point, and all of the upcoming points, it doesn't matter if you use the left or right side.

Tap on this point firmly and steadily, keeping your focus on the target. Hold that target issue in your mind. Then, while you continue to tap, say your reminder phrase.

For example, I've said my setup statement three times while tapping on the Karate Chop Point. I now transition to the next acupuncture point, tapping with two fingers at the beginning of my eyebrow. While I'm tapping, I say, "My fear of failure," honing my focus on the target and strengthening that connection. After that's done, I'm ready to move on to the next acupuncture point.

We're going to repeat the same process at the remaining acupuncture points.

Next up is the corner of the eye, towards the side of your head. Don't go too far back on your head-if you reach your temple, you've gone too far. We're aiming for the boney section next to where your eyelids come together. Again, tap on this section and repeat the reminder phrase.

After the corner of the eye, we tap underneath the eye. Specifically, we want to tap on a section of the bony orbit above the cheekbone but below your actual eyelid. Use the same two-finger tapping technique and repeat the reminder phrase once more.

The next meridian point we will use is the central part of your upper lip, right below your nose.

Once again, name the problem by repeating the reminder phrase before moving on.

Following the upper lip, we will move to the chin point. It's above your chin, below your lower lip, in the crease that forms between the two. Tap there, and say your reminder phrase. At this point, you're more than halfway through a tapping session!

The collarbone point comes next. This point, if you're familiar with acupuncture, is also known as K27. This is one of the few points where I recommend not using the two-finger technique. Instead, make a fist with your preferred hand. Tap that fist firmly, but not too hard, directly where you'd find the knot of a man's tie. This ensures that you'll cover at least one, if not both, of your collarbone points. Again, while you tap you should repeat the reminder phrase.

For the next point, imagine a seam running down the side of your body, splitting it perfectly in half. You'll need to tap on this seam, using the standard two-finger method, approximately four inches below your armpit. Repeat the reminder phrase as you do so, remaining focused on the target.

Last but not least is the top of the head. Tap directly on top, in a circular pattern. Repeat your reminder phrase one last time as you tap, and then you're done with tapping for your first session!

At the end of each round of tapping you'll want to pause, take a deep breath, hold it for a second or two, and then let it out. This lets the effects of the tapping really sink in before you lose focus on the target or move on.

Congratulations! You've finished your first treatment session!

Step Four-and-a-Half: Repeat

I didn't want to call this its own step, because it is a repeat of an earlier step. Nothing in this section should be particularly new to you, but it's essential to the process.

After you finish your first treatment session, you're going to return to step two from earlier: rating. Remember how I said the rating was important because it let us know whether or not we were making progress? This is when we establish our success.

Focus on your target once more. If possible, we want to remain focused on the target between back-to-back sessions so that we don't have to work too hard in reestablishing the flow of the EFT techniques. Keep the target at the forefront of your mind at all times.

Now, using the same principles we learned in step two, rate the target. Establish a number on the zero-to-ten scale that encapsulates how much discomfort or distress you associate with the target.

Is it higher? Lower? The same?

Hopefully, it's lower. That means that you made progress in the last session. Perhaps you made just a little progress. Maybe you made a significant amount of progress! Either way, you're on your way to dispelling the target's power over you.

If your rating is the same, it might mean you need a more refined setup statement. Perhaps the target you're focusing on has too little emotional resonance, or maybe it is too large for you to conquer all at once. As I said earlier, the setup statement is the hardest part of EFT. It's normal for you to need some practice, and you'll naturally get better as you become more in tune with your emotions. Just try to refocus, and then try again.

If your rating is higher, it could mean two things: either your earlier rating was lower than it should have been, or there are other angles that have come up from your subconscious.

Perhaps you rated your discomfort or distress too low in the initial step two phase, but this first treatment session has brought you more in touch with the problem and the accompanying emotions. Thus, when you rate the problem the second time, it suddenly seems more intense. This happens to my clients a lot, especially after the initial session. They need one good round of tapping before they can make an accurate self-assessment, and then the numbers tend to decrease with each subsequent round.

The other possibility-and this can happen whether your number is higher, lower, or the same-is that your initial round of tapping dredged up other angles of the problem from your subconscious. For instance, maybe you were focused on one symptom, but now you realize that the symptom actually stems from an event that took place a few months (or years) ago.

Eventually we want to resolve all of these other angles, too. If you're not making much progress in your main target, you may even want to resolve other angles *first,* in order to see if it helps chip away at the central problem. Treating one will help to treat the other. This also goes back to the idea that we want to relate everything to emotion, if possible. You may find that the other angles that arise during a session are far more emotionally resonant. This can be very helpful when addressing a stubborn issue, such as procrastination.

It's distinctly possible that you would never have been aware of these other angles consciously. It's only with the positive environment and stimulated meridians of a tapping session that they work their way to the surface, allowing us to treat them.

Regardless, we eventually want to get all our targets to zero. It's definitely possible, though, for some particularly stubborn traits or targets that you may want to consult a specialist. Still, repeat your treatment sessions until you're able to get those ratings as low as possible, eventually enabling you to move forward with your life.

The goal is to remove the charge on the problem. Whether it takes two sessions or ten, that's okay! Eventually, you'll be able to completely dispel the power of the target. The memories will remain, but they'll no longer be emotionally charged or emotionally resonant. You'll wonder how they ever held such control over your life. Why did you fear success? Why did you fear failure? It doesn't matter. You're a new person.

Release the conflict. Release the anxiety. Release the stress. Let the chi flow through your meridians. Let your body's electrical system return to normal.

Repeat steps one through four until you feel like you can go about your day normally.

It's an easy enough process to learn, but you'll still find its power surprising, even years after your first session. To this day, I'm still amazed by how incredibly elegant and efficient EFT is at clearing my mental roadblocks.

I guarantee that with a relatively low amount of time and effort, you can use EFT to eliminate your own procrastination.

Chapter 7

Sample Exercises

Although you now possess the basics to conduct your own EFT session, I understand that all of this can be a bit intimidating at the beginning. There are a lot of new concepts, a lot of ideas to consider, as well as memorizing those nine points.

I don't want to overwhelm you! This is easy, once you get the hang of it. I guarantee that you'll get all of this under your belt fairly quickly. In order to help expedite that process or to help anyone who feels a bit overwhelmed, this chapter is all about compiling examples of typical EFT sessions for your reference. Hopefully this will be useful if you're feeling stuck.

Regardless of the reason for your procrastination, I have included two examples of tapping sessions for each type of reason we've covered.

Don't feel like you're locked into these examples. For instance, the exercise in this chapter pertaining to fear of failure is just to get you started and comfortable with the program. Feel free to adapt any of these to your own needs. Use these sample sessions to get a feel for the process before you start creating your own.

I've compiled a list of the nine meridian points for you to glance at whenever you can't remember what comes next. Even though these were laid out for you in the last chapter, it's a bit lengthy for you to re-read whenever you can't remember one of the points.

Here are the points, in order:

1. Karate Chop Point
2. Eyebrow
3. Side of the Eye
4. Under Eye
5. Under Nose
6. Chin
7. Collarbone
8. Under Arm
9. Head

Be sure to run through those points as many times as you need until you have them all memorized. When it comes to tapping, we want the order of the points to come to us almost subconsciously. That way, you won't lose focus on the target because you have to stop and think about what point comes next.

You'll also get plenty of practice with the order of the acupuncture points if you follow any of the upcoming examples.

EXAMPLE 1: "The project isn't 'ripe' yet."

EXERCISE A

STEP 1: Choose a Target

The target is just the concept we're going to focus on in our tapping session. In this example, our procrastination springs from our inability to get a handle on the project. The project is something that we want to get done, but it feels like the project isn't "ripe" yet or ready to come out. We're working on getting rid of those feelings, so our target is going to relate to this particular stumbling block.

Moving forward with this example, our target is going to be:

"I feel stuck."

Everything that we do after this will relate to this initial target.

STEP 2: Rate The Intensity

Focus on the target. Turn the phrase, "I feel stuck," over in your mind, until you feel like you really have a handle on it.

Now, try to establish a baseline measurement of what that phrase means to you on a zero-to-ten scale (with zero the lowest intensity, ten the highest). How much discomfort or distress do you feel at being stuck?

This is an entirely subjective rating, so I can't tell you what to rate the target. Do you feel paralyzed by this "stuck" feeling? Maybe you're a ten. Maybe the feeling of being stuck is only interfering with your life a little bit, and you aren't too worried about it, but you'd still like to eliminate it. That might be a five or six.

As I said, it's entirely up to you. In fact, the numbers are only useful later on in the process, when we can compare them against other ratings you'll make. Don't stress about what the difference is between a six or a seven. Just give it your best shot at a fair rating.

STEP 3: Devise a Setup Statement

Perhaps the step that those new to EFT struggle with the most, crafting a setup statement that maximizes your session's efficiency requires a lot of practice. A good setup statement is half the battle.

Don't worry, if the setup statement in this example doesn't seem to do much for you. It's a pretty common starting point I use with clients who come to me feeling stuck, but we generally move on to narrower setup statements in later sessions. After a few sessions of EFT you'll have a

Get Your FREE 40 Minute Tapping Session: http://velocityhousepresents.com/stop-procrastinating

better idea what you should be concentrating on, and you can adapt the setup statement to your needs at that time.

For now, a good setup statement is:

"Even though I feel stuck and uninspired, I deeply and profoundly accept myself anyway."

Read it over a few times to get the wording down, and then we'll start tapping.

STEP 4: Tapping

We begin our session by tapping on the Karate Chop Point while saying the setup statement three times. It's worth noting that we don't necessarily repeat the same setup statement all three times. The concept stays the same, but we might vary the wording in order to further tune in to the target.

Begin tapping on the **Karate Chop Point**.

First time: *"Even though I feel stuck and uninspired, I deeply and profoundly accept myself anyway."*

Second: *"Even though I feel stuck and can't get this project done, I deeply and completely love and accept myself anyway."*

Third: *"Even though I feel stuck and can't move forward, I deeply and completely accept who I am and how I feel."*

After the setup statement, we tap on the series of acupuncture points in sequence. At each point, we also repeat the "reminder phrase." Like the setup statement, we vary the wording of the reminder phrase each time we say it, helping our brain stay focused on the target rather than getting bored and saying the words without any emotional resonance.

In order, then:

Eyebrow: *"I feel stuck."*
Side of the Eye: *"I feel so stuck."*
Under Eye: *"I can't get it done."*

Under Nose: *"I feel so uninspired."*
Chin: *"No wonder I feel stuck!"*
Collarbone: *"I feel stuck."*
Under Arm: *"I feel stuck."*
Head: *"I feel so stuck and uninspired."*

Now pause, take a deep breath, and let it out slowly. Let the session really sink in so the tapping can take effect.

Remain focused on the target, even though the tapping session is over, and re-rate the intensity of the target once again. Is it higher? Lower? The same?

Repeat these steps until your rating has decreased significantly (hopefully to zero), or until you come up with a new creative idea for how to finish your project. Good luck!

EXERCISE B

STEP 1: Choose a Target

The target for this exercise will be, *"I feel resistant to doing this project."* Notice how you feel resistant towards starting your work when you know that the project isn't ripe yet? We want to work out those feelings.

STEP 2: Rate the Intensity

Focus on the phrase, "I feel resistant to doing this project," and rate the intensity of your resistance. How hard is it for you to begin working? How much does your brain push back at the thought of starting your project?

STEP 3: Devise a Setup Statement

If you're resisting starting on a project, try this as a setup statement: *"Even though I have so much resistance to doing this project, I accept who I am and how I feel."* Study this statement before you move on to the next step.

Get Your FREE 40 Minute Tapping Session: *http://velocityhousepresents.com/stop-procrastinating*

STEP 4: Tapping

Begin by tapping on the Karate Chop Point and repeating the setup statement three times:

"Even though I have so much resistance to doing this project, I accept who I am and how I feel." "Even though I can't seem to get this project done, I accept who I am and how I feel."

"Even though I can't get myself to work on this project, I choose to accept who I am and how I feel." From there, begin tapping on the acupuncture points.

Eyebrow: *"I seem to be blocked."*
Side of the Eye: *"I feel so much resistance."*
Under Eye: *"I can't get myself to do the work."*
Under Nose: *"It's not ready yet."*
Chin: *"I can feel my resistance."*
Collarbone: *"It's not ready and neither am I!"*
Under Arm: *"It's not ready, and I feel so much resistance."*
Head: *"I can't get myself to work on this project."*

Now take a deep breath and measure the intensity of your feelings of resistance again, using our established scale. Repeat the tapping exercise as necessary.

Remember that the Law of Attraction hears our vibration, not our words. So now that your negative emotions related to being stuck and resistant are considerably lower, the Law of Attraction can read your more joyful, higher vibration, and you are in a position to attract more success and positive situations into your life.

EXAMPLE 2: Fear of Failure

EXERCISE A

STEP 1: Choose a Target

To choose a target, you have to know what the root of the issue is. Why are you procrastinating? What is the upside of procrastinating? What is the "reward" that your brain sees that allows you to procrastinate? This determines what we'll need to dispel during the tapping session.

For this example, we're going to go with a fairly common, though still very powerful, target: *"I'm afraid I'll be criticized."*

Of course, there are plenty of others you could use, but this is a great starting point if your procrastination stems from a fear of failure.

STEP 2: Rate the Intensity

Focus on the phrase *"I'm afraid I'll be criticized."*

Now measure how much fear you feel. How afraid are you of being criticized? How much discomfort or distress do you feel at the prospect?

It's subjective, so your rating is entirely your own. Once you're satisfied that you've properly rated the target, move on to the next step.

STEP 3: Devise a Setup Statement

If you're suffering from a fear of failure, and it's causing you to procrastinate, a great setup statement to start with is: *"Even though I'm afraid I'll be criticized if I complete the project, I deeply and completely love and accept myself anyway."*

Don't worry if you need to adjust this setup statement, either now or later. It's a foundation for you to build on and is simply one of the most common setup statements I use with newcomers before we delve further into their personal stumbling blocks. Get a good feel for the setup statement before you continue.

Get Your FREE 40 Minute Tapping Session: *http://velocityhousepresents.com/stop-procrastinating*

STEP 4: Tapping

Let's begin our session by tapping on the Karate Chop Point and repeating our variations of the setup statement. This will bring us in tune with the target and get our brain primed to experience the effects of EFT.

Now, begin tapping on the **Karate Chop Point.**

First time: *"Even though I'm afraid I'll be criticized if I complete the project, I deeply and completely love and accept myself anyway."*

Second: *"Even though I'm worried people will react negatively if I finish the project, I deeply andprofoundly love and accept myself anyway."*

Third: *"Even though I'm afraid I'll be criticized, I deeply and completely accept who I am and how I feel."*

After the setup statement, we tap on the series of acupuncture points in sequence, remembering to say the "reminder phrase" each step of the way in order to keep our brain tuned in and focused on the target.

In order, then:

Eyebrow: "I'm afraid I'll be criticized."
Side of the Eye: "I'm afraid I'll be criticized."
Under Eye: "I don't want to be criticized."
Under Nose: "I hate being criticized."
Chin: "I'm convinced they will criticize me."
Collarbone: "I don't want to be criticized…again."
Under Arm: "I'm convinced they will criticize me again."
Head: "I procrastinate, because I'm trying to avoid being criticized!"

After you've gone through all the points, take a deep breath and let it out slowly. Remain focused on the target, allowing the effects of the tapping session to take hold.

Now measure the target statement again, re-rating your fear.

Repeat these steps as many times as necessary until you are able to move forward with your project or your rating reaches zero.

Get Your FREE 40 Minute Tapping Session: *http://velocityhousepresents.com/stop-procrastinating*

EXERCISE B

STEP 1: Choose a Target

Getting a project done can be incredibly hard for a perfectionist, because it will never meet their exacting standards. For those instances, I recommend the following target: *"It has to be perfect."*

STEP 2: Rate the Intensity

Repeat the phrase, "it has to be perfect," aloud, and measure how true it feels to you, using the zero to ten point intensity scale. Are you obsessed with perfection? Is it holding you back from your potential?

STEP 3: Devise a Setup Statement

When you're battling against your own perfection, I find that a good initial setup statement is: *"Even though I'm procrastinating because I think my project has to be perfect, I accept all of me anyway."*

From there you can narrow things down to better fit your own circumstances, but this is a good place to begin.

STEP 4: Tapping

Begin by tapping on the Karate Chop Point while saying the three setup statements:

"Even though I'm procrastinating because I think my project has to be perfect, I accept all of me anyway."

"Even though it has to be perfect, so I can't get it done, I deeply and completely accept who I am." "Even though my perfectionism is getting in my way, I accept who I am anyway."

Now, begin tapping on the acupuncture points.

Eyebrow: "It has to be perfect"
Side of the Eye: "No wonder I'm procrastinating."

Get Your FREE 40 Minute Tapping Session: http://velocityhousepresents.com/stop-procrastinating

Under Eye: "It has to be perfect."
Under Nose: "No wonder I can't get it done."
Chin: "I'm afraid it won't be perfect."
Collarbone: "I know it won't be perfect."
Under Arm: "Then they'll reject it and me."
Head: "It has to be perfect, or I can't get it done."

Take a deep breath and measure the truth of the target again using the zero to ten point intensity scale. Repeat as necessary.

Now that your fears of being criticized and rejected have been considerably reduced through the tapping, your energy and vibration are naturally higher. This will allow you to automatically attract more of what you want into your life through the principles of Law of Attraction.

EXAMPLE 3: Fear of Success

From here on out I'm going to skip any background information and just provide you with the statements and actions you'll need to make it through the session. If anything is unclear, in terms of background information, I recommend reading through either the first or second examples in this chapter.

EXERCISE A

STEP 1: Choose a Target

Just like in the last example, you have to know what the root of the issue is before you can choose an effective target and clear out your procrastination. What are you gaining by procrastination, or what is it that your brain fears by completing (or even moving forward with) your project?

For this example our target will be: *"I don't want to rock the boat."*

You're afraid that your success will make waves amongst your family, friends or peers, and you are procrastinating in order to avoid this situation-even if that procrastination is to your detriment. This is a great starting point for you to build on later.

STEP 2: Rate the Intensity

Think about your target, "I don't want to rock the boat."

How much fear does the prospect of rocking the boat prompt in you? Rate that fear to quantify your own discomfort. Once again, this rating is entirely personal and subjective.

STEP 3: Devise a Setup Statement

If your fear of success is causing you to procrastinate, I've found that the following is a great setup statement to kick things off: *"Even though I'm afraid to rock the boat through achieving success, I deeply and completely love and accept myself anyway."*

When you have the setup statement down, you're ready to continue.

STEP 4: Tapping

The session starts when we tap on the Karate Chop Point and repeat three variations on the setup statement theme. This sets our brain up to receive the benefits or healing brought about by the EFT session.

When you're ready, start tapping on the **Karate Chop Point.**

First time: *"Even though I'm afraid to rock the boat through achieving success, I deeply and completely love and accept myself anyway."*

Second: *"Even though I'm afraid to rock the boat if I achieve my goals, I deeply and profoundly love and accept myself, anyway."*

Third: *"Even though I'm afraid to rock the boat in my personal or professional life, I deeply and completely accept who I am and how I feel."*

Next we tap on the acupuncture points in sequence. Don't forget to say the "reminder phrase" at each point.

Eyebrow: "I'm afraid my success will rock the boat."
Side of the Eye: "I'm afraid my success will rock the boat."
Under Eye: "I don't want to rock the boat."
Under Nose: "I don't want my success to rock the boat."
Chin: "I'm afraid I'll rock the boat with my success…so I procrastinate."
Collarbone: "I procrastinate so I don't have to be successful."
Under Arm: "I know it's not safe to rock the boat."
Head: "I'm afraid to rock the boat…no wonder I procrastinate!"

Now take a deep breath, and let it out slowly.

Measure the target statement again, re-rating your fear.

Repeat the session until you are able to move forward with your project or your rating reaches zero.

EXERCISE B

STEP 1: Choose a Target

The target for this exercise will be: *"I'm afraid to shine."*

STEP 2: Rate the Intensity

Think about your target, "I'm afraid to shine." How true does that statement feel? How intense are your feelings towards it? Rate those feelings on the zero to ten point intensity scale.

STEP 3: Devise a Setup Statement

When you're afraid to really stand out in your work, I find the following to be a good setup statement: *"Even though I'm afraid to shine, I deeply and completely love and accept myself anyway."*

STEP 4: Tapping

Start tapping on the Karate Chop Point while saying the setup statement three times:

"Even though I'm afraid to shine, I deeply and completely love and accept myself anyway."

"Even though I'm afraid to shine and it doesn't feel safe, I accept who I am and how I feel."

"Even though I'm afraid to shine by being successful, I deeply and completely accept who I am and how I feel."

Begin tapping on the acupuncture points.

Eyebrow: "I'm afraid to shine"
Side of the Eye: "I don't want to stand out"
Under Eye: "I'm afraid to shine"
Under Nose: "I don't want to stand out"
Chin: "I'm afraid to shine"
Collarbone: "They might hurt me if I shine"
Under Arm: "It's not safe to shine"
Head: "I'm afraid to shine"

Take a deep breath. Focus and measure the intensity of the target again, using the zero to ten point scale. Repeat if needed.

Now that your fears about standing out and being successful have been reduced or even erased through the tapping procedure, your vibration is automatically more joyful, relaxed and optimistic. This allows the Law of Attraction to deliver more success and abundance into your life.

Get Your FREE 40 Minute Tapping Session: *http://velocityhousepresents.com/stop-procrastinating*

EXAMPLE 4: Rebellion

If you skipped the previous examples and came straight to this one, I've dispensed with all but the most essential background information in the descriptions here. This only includes the phrases and actions you need to take in order to get through the session. Feel free to look back at exercises one through three if you feel confused or want more general information on the process.

EXERCISE A

STEP 1: Choose a Target

In order to choose an effective target, we need to know what is causing you to procrastinate. What does your brain think it gains by rebelling and putting off your work?

For this example, our target will be: *"I feel resentful. I'm tired of doing it **their** way"*

You're rebelling against deadlines, impositions, constrictions, and all the other trappings of a bureaucracy. Procrastination is your way of gaining back some control in your life. The only problem is that it's also hurting your relationships, whether personal or in your career. It's also making you unhappy, unhealthy, and resentful. You want to target these hostile, negative feelings and replace them with something more productive, hopefully getting your life back on track in the process.

This is a great target to start with, though you're free to change or adapt it whenever it's convenient or stops working for you.

STEP 2: Rate the Intensity

Focus on, "I feel resentful. I'm tired of doing it their way."

What kind of feelings does that statement conjure up? How much negativity do you feel? How resentful are you? Rate your emotions. Again, this rating is entirely subjective. It's up to you to make a rating that you feel comfortable with moving forward.

STEP 3: Devise a Setup Statement

If you're procrastinating out of resentment and rebellion, try starting off with this setup statement: *"Even though I feel resentful, and I'm tired of doing it their way, I deeply and completely accept myself."*

Not too hard, right? Make sure you have the setup statement down before moving on to the next step.

STEP 4: Tapping

Begin the session by tapping on the Karate Chop Point and repeating the three versions of the setup statement listed below.

Start tapping on the **Karate Chop Point** when you're ready.

First time: *"Even though I feel resentful, and I'm tired of doing it their way, I deeply and completely accept myself."*

Second: *"Even though I resent having to do it their way all the time, I deeply and profoundly love and accept myself anyway."*

Third: *"Even though I'm resentful and am tired of deadlines, I deeply and completely accept who I am and how I feel."*

After repeating the setup statement, we move on from the Karate Chop Point and begin to tap on the other acupuncture points in sequence. Remember to name the problem and say the "reminder phrase" when you reach each new point.

Eyebrow: "I feel resentful...I'm tired of meeting their deadlines."
Side of the Eye: "I want to do it my way."
Under Eye: "I feel resentful about their deadlines."
Under Nose: "I'm tired of meeting their deadlines."
Chin: "I feel so resentful."
Collarbone: "I'm tired of meeting their deadlines."
Under Arm: "I feel so resentful...I'm going to do it my way."
Head: "I'm going to do it my way."

Get Your FREE 40 Minute Tapping Session: http://velocityhousepresents.com/stop-procrastinating

When you're done with the last point, take a deep breath, and let it out slowly. Stay focused on the target, even as you relax.

Reanalyze the target, rating your feelings once again. Notice whether your rating increased, decreased, or stayed the same. Repeat the session until there is a significant decrease in your rating, or until you feel like you can move on with your project. Make sure to address any new angles that arise, as well.

EXERCISE B

STEP 1: Choose a Target

For this exercise, the target will be : *"I'm tired of being controlled by others."*

STEP 2: Rate the Intensity

Think about your target, *"I'm tired of being controlled by others."* Rate your feelings about the target on the zero to ten point intensity scale. How much truth is there to the target? Is it impacting your life?

STEP 3: Devise a Setup Statement

If you're being held back in your work or life because you're tired of being controlled by others, try using this setup statement to start: *"Even though I feel tired of being controlled by them, I accept who I am and how I feel."*

STEP 4: Tapping

Tap on the Karate Chop Point while repeating the three variations of the setup statement:

"Even though I feel tired of being controlled by them, I accept who I am and how I feel"

"Even though I feel tired of being controlled by others, I accept who I am and how I feel"

"Even though they're all trying to control me, I deeply and completely accept who I am"

Begin tapping on the acupuncture points.

Eyebrow: "I wish they'd stop controlling me."
Side of the Eye: "I don't want to be told what to do."
Under Eye: "Stop controlling me."
Under Nose: "I don't want to do it their way."
Chin: "Stop trying to control me!"
Collarbone: "They're always trying to control me."
Under Arm: "They always tell me what to do."
Head: "Stop trying to control me."

Take a deep breath and measure the intensity of the target, *"I'm tired of being controlled by others,"* again on the zero to ten point scale.

Now that you are no longer fighting the energy of your bosses or authority figures, no longer feeling so controlled by others, you can relax your vibration naturally, and attract more positive scenarios and situations into your life with the Law of Attraction.

I hope this chapter helped if you were feeling a bit lost or confused. Hopefully you now have a good understanding of how we choose targets, how we devise a setup statement and how the tapping session works.

You should also be well on your way to eliminating your procrastination. No matter what it is caused by, hopefully one of the four sets of exercises will help clear your mental blocks and get everything flowing again.

Like any good learning experience, however, there's more for you to do.

That's right. You've got homework to do.

Get Your FREE 40 Minute Tapping Session: *http://velocityhousepresents.com/stop-procrastinating*

Chapter 8

Homework

I can hear you already. "But Carol! Homework? I thought we were trying to *eliminate* my procrastination!"

We are! It'll be fun, I promise!

Plus, I've structured these homework lessons to remove any of your possible excuses. You can't say that the project isn't ready yet, because I'm about to tell you everything you need to know to complete it. You can't really fear failure or success, because nobody's ever going to know you did the project. You don't need to call me up and say, "Hey Carol, can you grade my homework?" If you fear failing yourself, or rocking the boat with yourself, don't. This is not that kind of project. There is no failing or succeeding. It's an ongoing process. That also means there's no deadline, so no real reason to rebel.

This homework consists of the same activities you've already done throughout this book; it is an extension of the process. If you've enjoyed the work we've done so far, or you've already seen its effects on your life, this is simply more of the same.

The homework is just to keep practicing your tapping. Make it a part of your life, even after you've eliminated your procrastination.

I'd recommend reviewing the sections of this book that really spoke to you. For instance, maybe you felt particularly drawn to the "Fear of Failure" or "Fear of Success" discussions. Go back and review them to see if you can draw more out of them. Use the sequences associated with those sections repeatedly, until those ideas no longer hold sway over you. Curb your fears.

Personally, I tap every day. I strongly recommend the same to everyone. You don't have to make a huge time commitment. A simple 5-15 minutes per day will keep your chi flowing and your body and mind in a healthy balance. No matter how good you get at EFT, your body will need maintenance. A quick tapping session each day can keep your emotional challenges considerably less charged, so you can continue moving forward.

Some excellent choices for your daily tapping targets:

- Daily stress
- Feeling overwhelmed
- Feeling powerless
- Feeling "unclear"

These problems have a way of creeping up on you over time, so addressing them when they're still small or barely formed is the best way of eliminating these issues altogether. You'll stay healthy and happy, both mentally and physically.

Remember to follow the simple four-step tapping process:

1. Choose a target. This can be an emotion, a belief, a symptom or an event. Just make sure it's something that holds significant emotional resonance in order to make effective use of EFT treatment.
2. Rate your negative feelings towards the target.
3. Devise your setup statement. "Even though I have this problem, I deeply and profoundly love and accept myself anyway."
4. Tap on the sequence of points while repeating the reminder phrase. Once completed, take a deep breath and re-rate your feelings on the target.

Get Your FREE 40 Minute Tapping Session: *http://velocityhousepresents.com/stop-procrastinating*

As I said earlier in the book, you can use EFT to address practically anything. As long as there's a

suitable target for you to focus on, try using tapping to clear the fears and mental blocks that sabotage you from the inside out. The more that you practice, the better you'll become at choosing the correct target, devising an efficient setup statement and dispelling those negative thoughts.

In order to hold yourself to a schedule, I recommend putting your daily tapping time into your calendar. This will help you remember to tap daily, but it's also a sign that you're making yourself a priority. Please, do so! Sometimes we need to put ourselves first in order to help others later. You can easily spare 5-15 minutes a day to take care of your body and mind. The rest of the day? Well, that's up to you. It's such a small commitment; it's easy to do, and it's worth every minute!

That's it! No more homework!

Well, not quite. There's one more thing:

Enjoy allowing more abundance, freedom and joy into your life.

Tapping is phenomenal. I strongly believe in the power of EFT. Yet learning to be more optimistic and grateful and allowing positivity into your lifestyle is also a big step.

In many cases, these mental blocks we later have to target and overcome are created from our own negativity. Stop these mental blocks before they even start! Focus on raising your vibration with appreciation and positivity, and you'll be amazed at the change in your lifestyle. Everything will seem so much richer.

I know, it can be hard. Even after all this time, I still sometimes struggle to keep a positive outlook. I've been tapping daily for over fifteen years. Nonetheless, I still end up with the occasional mental obstacle that needs to be cleared out. Life can be challenging, and we all need emotional maintenance!

Keep in mind that procrastination and these other mental blocks are normal. It's not the end of the world if you find yourself procrastinating. It's just something that happens. There's nothing wrong with you, or at least nothing that can't be fixed. The problem comes from not addressing the real problem-the solution procrastination gives you (avoiding criticism, fearing that your success will rock the boat, taking your power back, etc.). Don't let it fester. Don't let your fears rule you.

You now know how to take care of these mental blocks, how to reset your body's chi and how to think positively. In other words, you have all the tools you need. If something particularly stubborn comes up, feel free to seek outside help. I have coached and trained highly skilled practitioners and have other materials you're welcome to look into.

Still, you have all that you need to eradicate bad habits and turn your life around. You've learned how to use EFT tapping, which I dare say, is one of the most important and efficient skills you can master in order to transform your life. Your continued practice of EFT will serve to enrich and improve your life. It doesn't just stop with procrastination. You have the knowledge to make a positive difference in your life.

Now, get out there and make use of it!
Enjoy increased productivity and abundance!

Get Your FREE 40 Minute Tapping Session: *http://velocityhousepresents.com/stop-procrastinating*

Made in the USA
San Bernardino, CA
08 September 2013